SHREWSBURY TO LUDLOW

Vic Mitchell and Keith Smith

Front cover: LMS 2-8-0 no. 48665 plods south through Craven Arms with a heavy freight train on 10th September 1949. (H.C.Casserley)

Back cover: Two national icons were recorded at Shrewsbury in 1996: the Abbey church and the LNWR's impressive signal box. (M.J.Stretton)

Published February 2008

ISBN 978 1 906008 21 5

Design Deborah Esher
Typesetting Barbara Mitchell

Published by
    Middleton Press
    Easebourne Lane
    Midhurst
    West Sussex
    GU29 9AZ
Tel: 01730 813169
Fax: 01730 812601
Email: info@middletonpress.co.uk
www.middletonpress.co.uk

Printed & bound by Biddles Ltd, Kings Lynn

BRANCHES

INDEX

I. Railway Clearing House map with the halts and the BCR added.

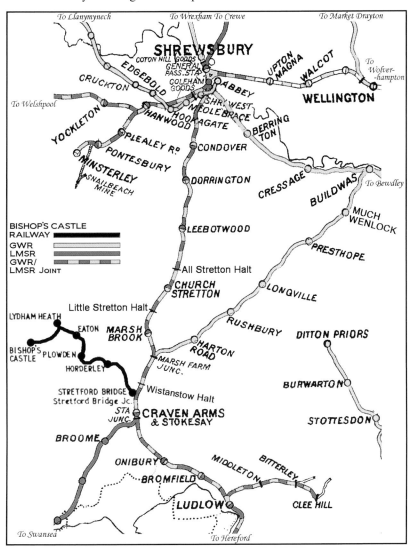

ACKNOWLEDGEMENTS

We are very grateful for the assistance received from many of those mentioned in the credits also to D.Askew, W.R.Burton, C.L.Caddy, A.R.Carder, L.Crosier, G.Croughton, M.Dart, J.C.Gillham, S.C.Jenkins, N.Langridge, K.Lucas, Mr D. and Dr S.Salter, and in particular, our always supportive wives, Barbara Mitchell and Janet Smith.

GEOGRAPHICAL SETTING

Our journey is entirely within Shropshire and begins aptly at its county town, Shrewsbury. On more than ¾ of the town's boundary is the River Severn, which gave it a good defensive position. (The castle is adjacent to the station.)

The route is generally on a rising gradient as far as Church Stretton and runs close to the Cound Brook between Condover and Dorrington, passing over mainly Limestone.

The geology becomes complex south of Leebotwood, where the line is flanked by impressive ridges on both sides, for about four miles. The valley of the River Onny is joined one mile north of Craven Arms; it accommodated the eastern half of the Bishop's Castle Railway in a deep incision.

The river flows into the River Teme at Bromfield and the line passes over another tributary of it, the River Corve, on its approach to Ludlow. North of the town, the mineral line to Clee Hill branched off eastwards to reach important deposits of Dhustone, at over 1200ft above sea level.

The maps are to the scale of 25ins to 1 mile, with north at the top, unless otherwise indicated.

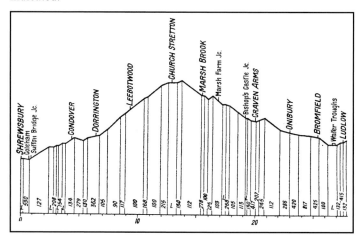

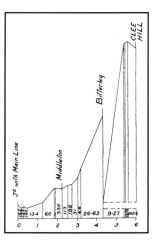

HISTORICAL BACKGROUND

Shrewsbury was served by the Shrewsbury & Chester Railway from 1848, the Shrewsbury & Birmingham Railway from 1849, the line north to Whitchurch from 1858 and one to Welshpool from 1862.

The Shrewsbury & Hereford Railway opened south to Ludlow on 21st April 1852 and on to Hereford on 6th December 1853. Known as the "North & West Route", it became the joint property of the London & North Western Railway, the Great Western Railway and the West Midland Railway on 1st July 1862. Originally single track, the route was steadily doubled. The WMR became part of the GWR in August 1863. The Severn Valley Railway to Hartlebury opened in 1862.

The Ludlow & Clee Hill Railway ran from 24th August 1864 and came under GWR/LNWR joint ownership in 1893. The complex story of the independent line west from Shrewsbury is touched upon in map captions III and IV, but it was only in its final years connected to our route.

The Knighton Railway was opened from Craven Arms in 1860-61 and joined the Central Wales Railway in 1862. (The route is still in use.)

The Bishop's Castle Railway from Craven Arms came into use on 24th October 1865 and was intended to serve Montgomery from a junction at Lydham Heath (see map I). However, this line was never built and all trains had to reverse here. The company remained independent, but was insolvent for most of its life.

A branch eastwards was opened in 1867 by the Wenlock Railway, this becoming part of the GWR in 1896.

The LNWR was responsible for the signalling of the main line until 1st January 1904, when the GWR took over.

The LNWR became part of the London Midland & Scottish Railway in 1923, but the GWR retained its identity. A joint operation of the North and West Route continued until nationalisation in 1948, when all lines in the area became part of the Western Region of British Railways.

Dates of withdrawal of passenger services on the branches from the main lines are:

Bishop's Castle	20th April 1935
Much Wenlock	31st December 1951
Bewdley (Severn Valley)	9th September 1963

The Clee Hill branch closed on 7th November 1960. Cessation of other freight traffic is detailed in the captions.

Privatisation in 1996 resulted in South Wales & West providing services ("South" was dropped in 1998). However, after reorganisation in 2001, Wales & Borders became the franchisee. Arriva Trains Wales took over in December 2003.

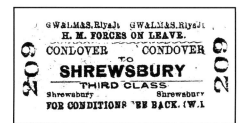

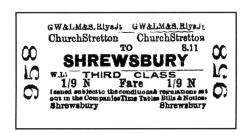

PASSENGER SERVICES

Down trains are southbound and those running on at least five days per week are described below, with the Sunday frequency shown in brackets. Initially, Ludlow received four trains from Shrewsbury and there were seven (2) to Hereford for most of the 1860s.

The 1890 timetable showed nine (3), plus one to Craven Arms. Four of these were expresses.

In 1915 there were 11 (2) trains serving Ludlow, with four more as far as Craven Arms.

Below is the number of trains serving Ludlow. Trains calling at all stations are in brackets.

	Weekdays	Sundays
1930	10 (7)	3 (0)
1950	9 (4)	3 (0)
1970	6	2
1990	14	4
2007	26	10

These figures exclude trains to the Central Wales (now Heart of Wales) line.

Bishop's Castle Railway

For most of the life of the line, there were three trains, weekdays only.
However, in the final years the middle trip did not run on Tuesdays and Thursdays.

The column heading "gov" refers to cheap fares issued with "Parliamentary" tickets. These were charged at one penny per mile, under Gladstone's Act of 1844. Some examples of such tickets are shown herein.

Sec., William Wilding.] BISHOP'S CASTLE. [Traffic Man., John Craston.

Miles	Fares 1 cl. s. d.	2 cl. s. d.	3 cl. s. d.	Down.	1,2,3 mrn	1&2 aft	1,2,3 aft		
				Bishop's Castle ....dep	9 30	1235	5 0	....	....
2¼	0 6	0 4	0 2	Lydham Heath........	9 45	1245	5 10	....	....
4	....	....	....	Eaton	a	....	a	....	....
5¼	1 3	0 10	0 5	Plowden	9 55	1257	5 20	....	....
7½	1 9	1 2	0 7	Horderley	10 5	1 5	5 30	....	....
10¾	2 9	1 10	0 10½	Craven Arms 128, 15 a	1020	1 15	5 45	....	....

Miles	Fares 1 cl. s. d.	2 cl. s. d.	3 cl. s. d.	From Shrewsbury and Hereford, see below.	1,2,3 mrn	1&2 aft	1,2,3 aft		
				Craven Arms......dep	1055	2 30	6 50	....	....
3¼	....	....	....	Horderley	11 5	2 40	7 5	....	....
5¾	....	....	....	Plowden	1120	2 50	7 15	....	....
6¾	....	....	....	Eaton	a	....	a	....	....
8¾	....	....	....	Lydham Heath.... ...	1130	3 10	7 35	....	....
10¾	2 9	1 10	0 10	Bishop's Castle ....arr	1145	3 15	7 40	....	....

a Stop when required.

No Sunday Trains.

December 1

BISHOP'S CASTLE and CRAVEN ARMS AND STOKESAY.—Bishop's Castle.
Receiver and Manager, T. Cartwright.

Miles	Down.	Week Days only. mrn		gov	aft	aft	
	Bishop's Castle ....dep.	6 55	Runs on Bishop's Castle Fair Days only.	9 0	1230	5 35	....
2¼	Lydham Heath	7 3		9 10	1240	5 45	....
4	Eaton......................	Sig.		Sig.	Sig.	f	....
5¼	Plowden....................	7 13		9 25	1250	5 55	....
7¾	Horderley	Sig.		Sig.	Sig.	Sig.	....
9¾	Stretford Bridge J. [488, 492	Sig.		Sig.	Sig.	Sig.	....
10½	Craven Arms & Stokesvarr.	7 30		9 45	1 10	6 15	....

Miles	Up.	Week Days only. mrn		mrn	aft	gov
	Craven Arms & Stokesaydep	7 45	Runs on Bishop's Castle Fair Days only.	1115	3 10	6 55
1	Stretford Bridge Junction...	Sig.		Sig.	Sig.	Sig.
3	Horderley	Sig.		Sig.	Sig.	Sig.
5	Plowden	8 5		1135	3 25	7 15
6½	Eaton	Sig.		f	Sig.	Sig.
8¼	Lydham Heath	8 18		1148	3 38	7 25
10½	Bishop's Castle.........arr.	8 25		12 0	3 50	7 35

f Stops on Fridays only.

August 1915

November 1

BISHOP'S CASTLE and CRAVEN ARMS AND STOKESAY.—Bishop's Castle.

Miles	Down.	Week Days only. mrn		Z		aft		
	Bishop's Castle..........dep.	9 20	....	1240	....	5 30	....	....
2¼	Lydham Heath..............	9 30	....	1250	....	5 40	....	....
4	Eaton.......................	Aa	....	Aa	....	Aa	....	....
5¼	Plowden....................	9 45	....	1 10	....	5 50	....	....
7¾	Horderley..................	Aa	....	Aa	....	Aa	....	....
9¾	Stretford Bridge J. [486,488	Aa	....	Aa	....	Aa	....	....
10½	Craven Arms & Stokesayarr	1010	....	1 30	....	6 20	....	....

Miles	Up.	Week Days only. mrn		Z		aft		
	Craven Arms & Stokesaydep	1120	....	3 15	....	7 5	....	....
¾	Stretford Bridge Junction...	Aa	....	Aa	....	Aa	....	....
3	Horderley....................	Aa	....	Aa	....	Aa	....	....
5	Plowden	1140	....	3 30	....	7 25	....	....
6½	Eaton........................	Cc	....	Aa	....	Aa	....	....
8¼	Lydham Heath...............	1153	....	3 43	....	7 35	....	....
10½	Bishop's Castle.........arr.	12 5	....	3 55	....	7 45	....	....

NOTES.

Aa Stop when required.
Cc Stops on Fridays only on notice being given to the Guard.
Z Mons., Fris., and Sats.

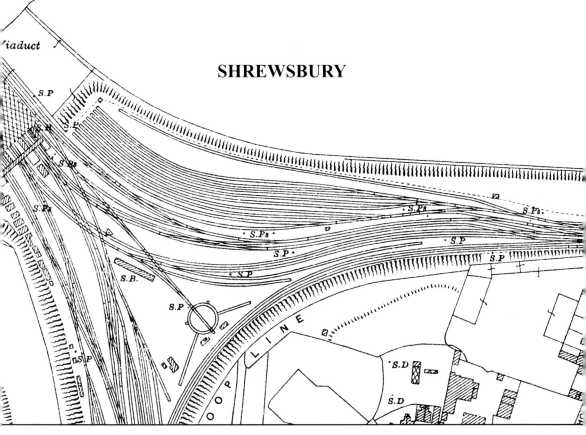

SHREWSBURY

II.   The 1927 map has the River Severn and part of the station roof top left. Our route is at the bottom and the Wellington line is on the right. The Loop Line had been opened on 1st May 1867 and was used mainly for freight traffic.

1.   A joint station was provided from the outset and was recorded in 1849, along with part of the castle. The former was extended on the left in 1854 and further alterations took place in 1861-63. Major changes followed in 1900-01 when the approach road was lowered, the cellars were opened up, more rooms were constructed and a subway added. (A.Dudman coll.)

← 2. The present platform numbering dates from 1950 and standing at no. 6 on 14th April 1962 is no. 1016 *County of Hants* with the 5.10pm stopping train to Wolverhampton Low Level. The overall roof was mostly dismantled by 1964. (J.Langford)

← 3. Initially passengers crossed the tracks on the level, but the public footbridge was eventually provided with steps to the platforms. Known as the "The Dana", it is evident here. The later footbridge (shown on the map) lasted until 1961.
(Lens of Sutton coll.)

4.   Seen from the end of platform 4 on 16th June 1962 is the massive 180-lever signal box, which was of LNWR origin. The locomotive is 4-6-0 no. 6901 *Arley Hall*.
(D.K.Jones)

5.　　The southward continuation of the same staff crossing is seen two weeks later, as no. 1025 *County of Radnor* shunts empty stock. The locomotive on the left is within the triangular junction, near the site of the turntable. (B.W.L.Brooksbank)

→　6. The prison overlooks the station and the long Dana footbridge. Standing on the bridge over the River Severn on 15th August 1984 are nos 31308 and 47471. The latter is at platform 7 with the 19.49 to Euston. (D.H.Mitchell)

→　7. No. 40109 is running south on 6th April 1974 with oil tanks, while a DMU waits at platform 5, one of two bay platforms commonly used by local and Central Wales trains. Platforms 4 and 7 could accommodate fifteen coaches, platforms 5 and 6 five, and 3 thirteen. (T.Heavyside)

8.   This view from 8th August 1990 features the up starting signals at platform 4 and the two bay platforms. The train is the 12.50 departure for Wolverhampton and the building on the right is the historic Abbey church. (V.Mitchell)

→ 9. Recorded on the same day is the 12.43 to Chester, about to hammer its way over the crossings. The lofty Severn Bridge junction box was still in use in 2008. (V.Mitchell)

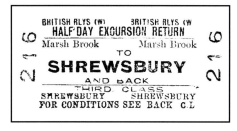

→ 10. The date is 12th September 1992 and no. 37710 is taking the Down Main with a train of steel coils from Llanwern to Shotton. This line has no platform. (T.Heavyside)

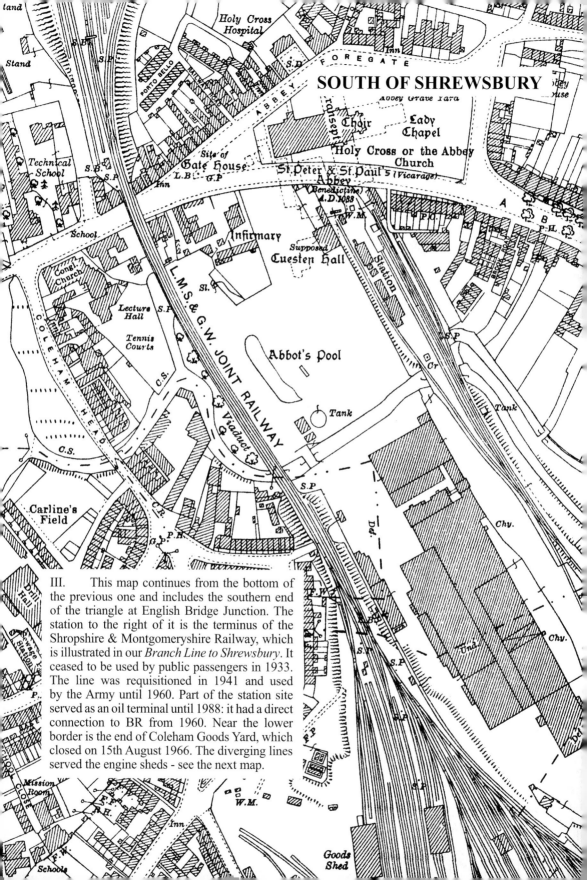

SOUTH OF SHREWSBURY

III.   This map continues from the bottom of the previous one and includes the southern end of the triangle at English Bridge Junction. The station to the right of it is the terminus of the Shropshire & Montgomeryshire Railway, which is illustrated in our *Branch Line to Shrewsbury*. It ceased to be used by public passengers in 1933. The line was requisitioned in 1941 and used by the Army until 1960. Part of the station site served as an oil terminal until 1988: it had a direct connection to BR from 1960. Near the lower border is the end of Coleham Goods Yard, which closed on 15th August 1966. The diverging lines served the engine sheds - see the next map.

English Bridge Junction

11.   Class 3521 4-4-0 no. 3557 is running from the south sometime in 1929 and is near the bottom of map II. The signal gantry is at the top of map III and south of it is English Bridge Junction signal box. It had a 23-lever frame fitted in 1914 and closed in 1955. (Kidderminster Railway Museum)

Coleham

12.   Moving south, we see no. 5054 *Earl of Ducie* passing the entrance to Coleham Goods Yard (left) on 29th April 1956, with part of the Abbey church above the cab. Coleham signal box had 30 levers from 1916 and closed on 2nd April 1967. (G.Adams/M.J.Stretton coll.)

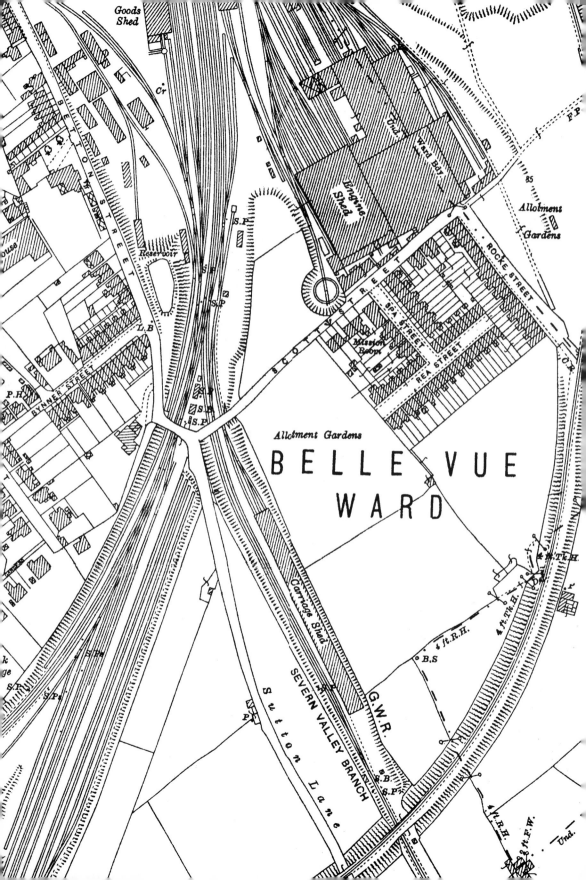

← IV. This map overlaps the previous one and has our route curving to the lower left corner, with the line to Welshpool running to the left border, from Sutton Bridge Junction. Also diverging there is the Severn Valley line and passing over that is the S&MR. This had evolved from the Potteries, Shrewsbury & North Wales Railway, which had curved away to the right to join the line to Wellington, between 1866 and 1880. The building marked Engine Shed was built by the LNWR in 1877 and the structure to the east of it was the GWR locomotive roundhouse of 1880. North of that is Coleham Wagon Works. The 50ft turntable had been provided by the LNWR and it was replaced by a 70ft one.

Shrewsbury Engine Shed

13. The ex-LNWR part of the shed was recorded in August 1956; nearest is no. 6872 *Crawley Grange*, with no. 5917 *Westminster Hall* and no. 7819 *Hinton Manor* also in view. The shed code was 84G at that time. (D.K.Jones)

14. A photograph of the former GWR side in 1960 includes no. 5032 *Usk Castle* and no. 5038 *Morlais Castle*. The code was 6D from September 1963, when the London Midland Region took control of Coleham shed and also the route south to within one mile of Craven Arms. (D.K.Jones)

15. Major changes took place following the end of steam here in March 1967. Diesel shunters had begun to appear in the late 1950s, with "Westerns" and then "Warships" following in the 1960s. This is the scene on 5th September 1971, when class 47 nos 1696 and 1707 were present and the sheds were in terminal decline. (D.H.Mitchell)

Sutton Bridge Junction

↓ 16. From left to right in this May 1957 northward panorama we see the goods shed, six sidings, two running lines, the coaling plant and Coleham locomotive depot. Lower left is the Severn Valley line. (F.Hornby)

↑   17. Much had been cleared away by April 1974, but the same signals can be seen again. No. D125 is on the foot crossing used by signalmen to access the tablet catcher on the white post. The signal box is to the right of the camera and was still in use in 2008. The GWR had fitted it with a 63-lever frame in 1913. (T.Heavyside)

18.   A different angle from the same bridge on 17th July 1976 features no. 47159 with the 09.25 Manchester to Penzance. The goods shed was still standing, although the goods yard had closed on 15th August 1966. Several sidings remained in use by the engineers, more than 20 years later. (T.Heavyside)

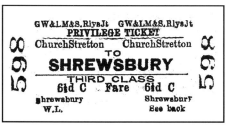

South of Sutton Bridge Junction

19.   A southward panorama from the bridge on the same day has the single line to Welshpool curving to the right and the double track to Ludlow to the left of the freight train, which is on the goods loop behind no. 47104. (T.Heavyside)

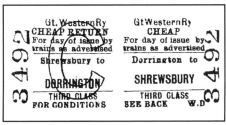

← 20. The 10.04 Cardiff to Manchester was worked by no. 150235 on 20th May 1989 and is seen through the balustrade of the bridge visible in the background of the previous picture. The sidings on the right of it connect to the main line near this train. (T.Heavyside)

↓ 21. The route was the first to experience the regular return of steam in 1972. No. 35028 *Clan Line* accelerates the "Welsh Marches Express" southwards on 10th November 1984. One window of Sutton Bridge Junction box is in the distance. (H.Ballantyne)

→ 22. No. 37426 *Y Lein Fach/Vale of Rheidol* is hauling the 09.15 Liverpool to Cardiff on 1st October 1988. In the background is Bayston Hill Quarry, which had a siding controlled by a GWR signal box with 16 levers. (T.Heavyside)

↘ 23. In Railfreight livery, no. 37904 runs south on 19th June 1987 with empty steel coil wagons from Dee Marsh to Cardiff Tidal Sidings. (H.Ballantyne)

CONDOVER

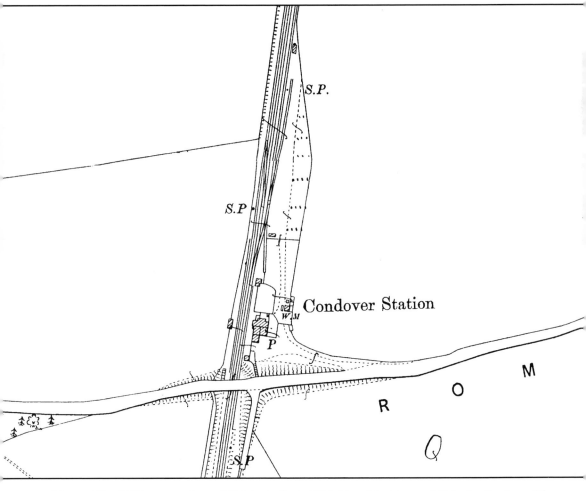

V.   The 1902 survey shows WM to indicate Weighing Machine and P is for Postbox. The population was 1638 in 1901.

24.   An Edwardian postcard features a small hip-roofed signal box and low platforms. Both were altered before the next photograph was taken, by which time an extension had been added. Goods loops were in use north of the station in 1941-66. (Stations UK)

25.   A train stands on the down goods loop in 1955, while two wagons occupy the parallel siding. The cattle pen was behind the 33-lever ex-GWR signal box, which closed on 12th March 1967. Passenger service ceased on 9th June 1958 and freight on 7th October 1963. (Stations UK)

DORRINGTON

VI. The 1902 survey reveals that a small cattle market was developed near the station. The signal box (S.B.) had a LNWR 15-lever frame in use from about 1900 to 1941.

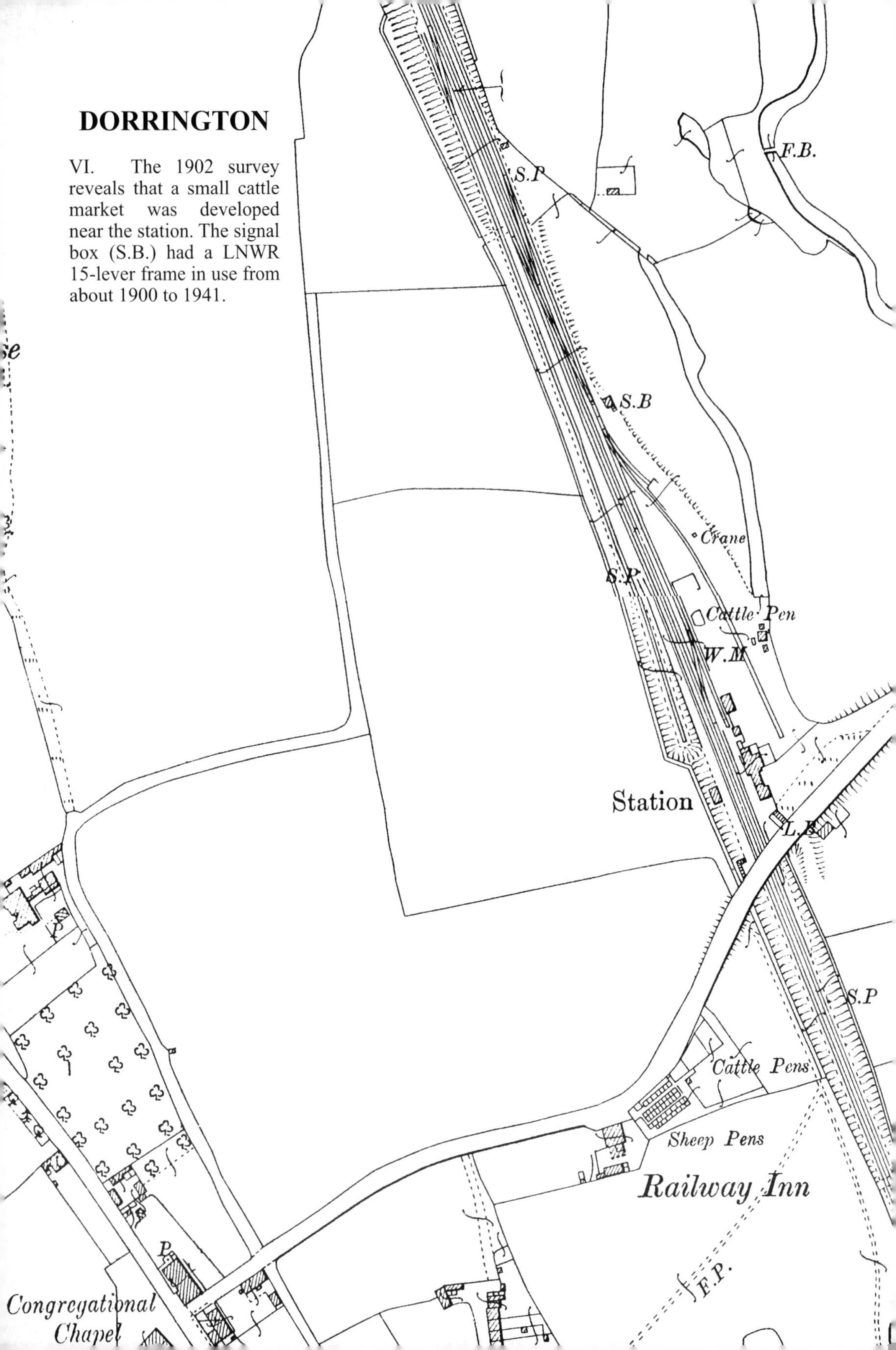

F.B.

S.P

S.B

Crane

S.P

Cattle Pen

W.M

Station

L.B

S.P

Cattle Pens

Sheep Pens

Railway Inn

F.P.

Congregational Chapel

26.   The main buildings were photographed in 1955, as authority approaches. There had been a wagon turntable at the far end of the platform in the 19th century. (Stations UK)

27.   A solitary passenger is near the waiting shelter as an up train calls, sometime in 1955. The tiny goods shed was supplemented by a grounded van body. (Stations UK)

28.   An extra siding was added in 1936 for milk traffic and a new crane of six-ton capacity was provided in a fresh position. Ex-LMS no. 45505 *The Royal Army Ordnance Corps* was shunting six-wheeled milk tankers on 22nd March 1958. (G.Adams/M.J.Stretton coll.)

29.   Passenger service was withdrawn on 9th June 1958 and the photograph was taken on 18th May 1961. The down refuge siding had been a loop from 1942 to 1959. (R.G.Nelson/T.Walsh)

30.   The goods shed and one siding remained to be photographed on 3rd July 1983, as no. 5051 *Earl Bathurst* sped south with the "Red Dragon". The GWR had fitted the box with a 33-lever frame in 1941. (H.Ballantyne)

31.   The 09.14 Cardiff to Liverpool service was worked by Sprinter no. 156467 on 9th May 1989. Semaphore signals were still controlled from the local box in 2008. (P.G.Barnes)

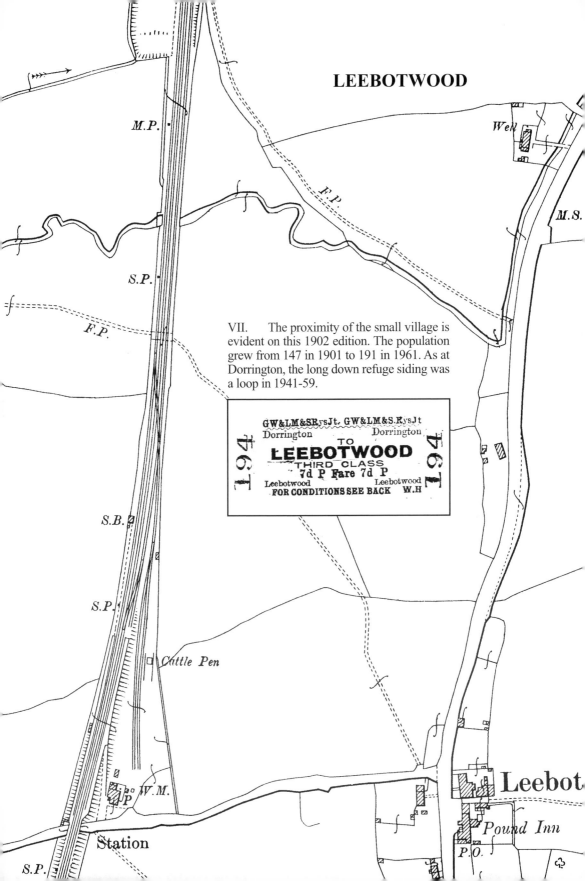

LEEBOTWOOD

M.P.

Wel

F.P.

M.S.

S.P.

F.P.

VII. The proximity of the small village is evident on this 1902 edition. The population grew from 147 in 1901 to 191 in 1961. As at Dorrington, the long down refuge siding was a loop in 1941-59.

194   GW&LM&SRysJt. GW&LM&S.RysJt
Dorrington   Dorrington
TO
LEEBOTWOOD
THIRD CLASS
7d P Fare 7d P
Leebotwood   Leebotwood
FOR CONDITIONS SEE BACK   W.H   **194**

S.B.

S.P.

Cattle Pen

W.M.

P

Station

S.P.

Leebot

Pound Inn

P.O.

32.   The station building is on the right, but the path up to the down platform is hidden by the trees. Access to the up platform was under the road bridge and up two flights of stairs. This is a 1955 view. (Stations UK)

33.   Both passenger and freight services were withdrawn on 9th June 1958, staffing having ceased on 2nd July 1956. In the distance is the signal box, which had 22 levers and lasted until 15th October 1967. The photograph is from May 1961. Two miles to the south was All Stretton Halt from 29th February 1936 until 9th June 1958, although it was closed from 4th January 1943 until 6th May 1946. (R.G.Nelson/T.Walsh)

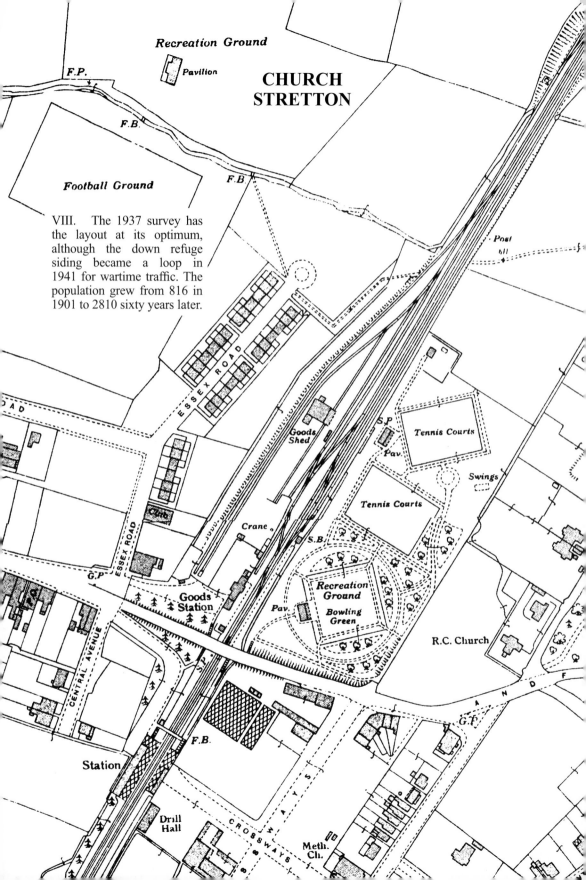

Recreation Ground

Pavilion

CHURCH STRETTON

F.P.

F.B.

Football Ground

VIII. The 1937 survey has the layout at its optimum, although the down refuge siding became a loop in 1941 for wartime traffic. The population grew from 816 in 1901 to 2810 sixty years later.

F.B.

F.B.

Post hll

ESSEX ROAD

ESSEX ROAD

Goods Shed

S.P.

Pav.

Tennis Courts

Swings

Tennis Courts

Club

ROAD

Crane

S.B.

G.P.

Goods Station

Recreation Ground

Pav.

Bowling Green

R.C. Church

CENTRAL AVENUE

S.P.

G.P.

Station

F.B.

Drill Hall

CROSSWAYS

Meth. Ch.

A Y S

34.   The first station was north of the road bridge, although its low platforms were extended under it. An entirely new station to the south of it opened on 23rd May 1914. (M.J.Stretton coll.)

35.   The replacement was provided with generous glazed canopies indicated with diamonds on the map. DMUs displaying cats whiskers were common on the route from 1958. (Stations UK)

36.   This is a 1961 southward view; staffing ceased on 3rd July 1967 and the buildings were soon demolished. (R.G.Nelson/T.Walsh)

→   37. The goods yard had closed on 19th September 1966 and just the dock siding remained on 17th July 1976. An express DMU speeds south forming the 12.08 Crewe to Cardiff. The original station (left) served as the stationmasters residence for many years and is now a private dwelling. (T.Heavyside)

→   38. No. 6000 *King George V* was based at Hereford and worked many specials on the route. Running wrong line on 3rd July 1977, it is passing under one of the electrically lit semaphore signals. Both distant signals were colour lights. (D.T.Rowe)

39.　　No. 37710 heads a train of steel coils on 4th July 1989 and passes under the roofless footbridge. Bus shelters were available for passenger protection. (P.G.Barnes)

40.　　The 1872 signal box was recorded on the same day. The trackbed through Church Stretton and the signal box locking room were flooded in November 2000 when a culvert became blocked during a heavy storm. Following the damage done to the box, it remained switched out and in January 2004 all signal arms were removed with the box becoming formally abolished; it had a 25-lever frame installed in 1890. A 2½ ton goods crane had once been opposite the box. Little Stretton Halt was 1¼ miles south of the station and was open from 18th April 1935. Closure dates were as for All Stretton Halt. (P.G.Barnes)

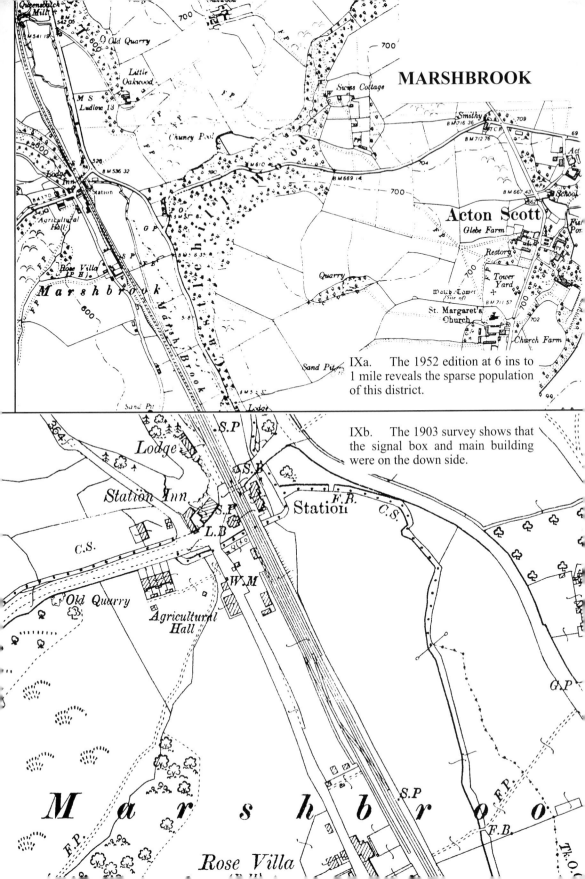

MARSHBROOK

IXa.   The 1952 edition at 6 ins to 1 mile reveals the sparse population of this district.

IXb.   The 1903 survey shows that the signal box and main building were on the down side.

41.   A northward view in the early 1950s features the up waiting shelter, which was of generous proportions, in view of the small number of inhabitants in the vicinity. (R.S.Carpenter)

→ 42. A southbound freight is about to pass the staff transport parked on the platform in 1955. Passenger service here ceased on 9th June 1958. The brook passes under the tracks and platforms below the barrow. (Stations UK)

GW&LM&SRysJt GW&LM&SRysJt
Marsh Brook   Marsh Brook
TO
CHURCH STRETTON
THIRD CLASS
4½d Fare 4½d
Issued subject to the conditions&regulations set
out in theCompaniesTimeTablesBills&Notices
Church Stretton   Church Stretton

6907 6907

→ 43. A 1961 panorama is from the goods platform; the others had been removed. Goods traffic at this yard came to an end on 2nd December 1963. There was a 3-ton crane listed in 1938. (R.G.Nelson/T.Walsh)

44.   Approaching the level crossing on 17th July 1976 is no. L707 working the 11.35 Cardiff to Crewe. It is seen from the signal box. The complex rodding is for gate movement. (T.Heavyside)

45.   This photograph from May 2001 includes full lifting barriers and the station building in use as a dwelling. The signal box at Marsh Farm Junction, for Much Wenlock, was 1¼ miles to the south. It had 36 levers from 1903. (B.W.L.Brooksbank)

WISTANSTOW HALT

46.   The nearby 10-lever signal box closed in 1933 and the halt opened on 7th May 1934. It remained in use until 11th June 1956. (Lens of Sutton coll.)

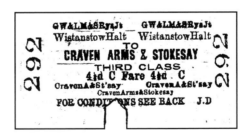

Bishop's Castle Railway

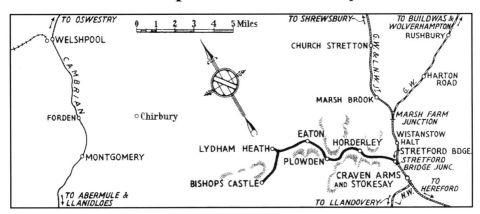

X.   The line was built with the minimum expenditure and it always used secondhand and life expired equipment. Revenue was poor and bankruptcy came within months of opening. The railway closed completely for a period in 1867. The same happened again in 1877, due to a dispute with the Receiver over land not paid for. A second attempt to build a connection to Montgomery (left) was made in 1884 and a third in 1923. The company was in receivership until closed by the High Court in 1935. (Railway Magazine)

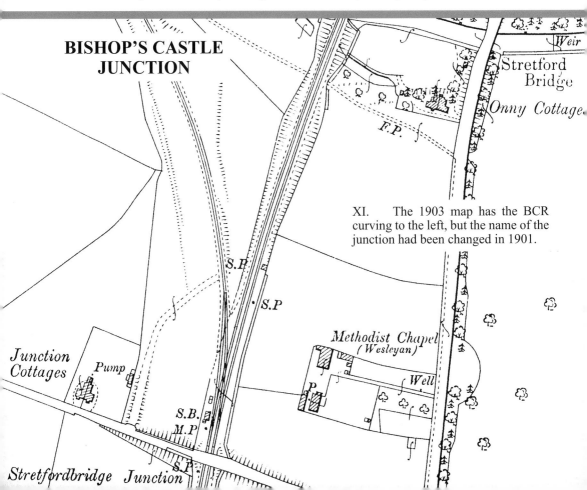

BISHOP'S CASTLE JUNCTION

XI.   The 1903 map has the BCR curving to the left, but the name of the junction had been changed in 1901.

47.   The signal box had 25 levers and was in use until about February 1937, although the BCR had closed on 20th April 1935. Access to the halt was across the field in the centre of this 1931 photograph. (R.S.Carpenter coll.)

48.   A photograph from 26th July 1936 includes evidence of double track; this extended for about 50yds until 1892. The second track was to the left of the point rodding, seen on the right. (R.S.Carpenter coll.)

49. The final movement on the BCR was recorded on 21st February 1937, as its 0-6-0 *Carlisle* left the line with the demolition train. The loco was cut up at Craven Arms. (F.C.Nicholas/ GWR Magazine)

STRETFORD BRIDGE HALT

50. The field referred to in caption 47 is on the right. Passengers crossed it and the track to reach the halt, which is shown on the map as a single line. The halt first appeared in timetables in May 1890 and it was photographed in July 1936. (R.S.Carpenter coll.)

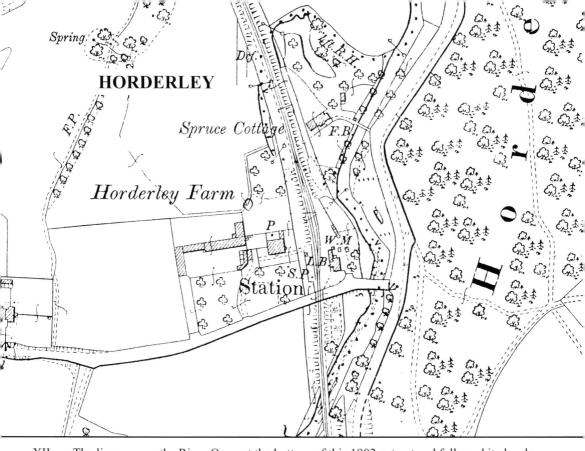

XII.　　The line crosses the River Onny at the bottom of this 1902 extract and followed it closely in a steep sided valley for over four miles.

51.　　One of the BCR economy measures was in signal post ladders. One could be carried to the lamps when fresh oil and wick trimming was required. Hence the low location of the spectacles. This was a request stop periodically in the final 20 years. (R.M.Casserley coll.)

52.   Passengers ambled over the tracks from the main building to reach the platform. There was a GPO letter box in the wall of the former, even after closure. The meaning of "lean-to" is evident. (R.M.Casserley coll.)

53.   All areas were overgrown and there were few travellers to be concerned. This was the ultimate neglected railway at the time of closure and also for long before. (Stations UK)

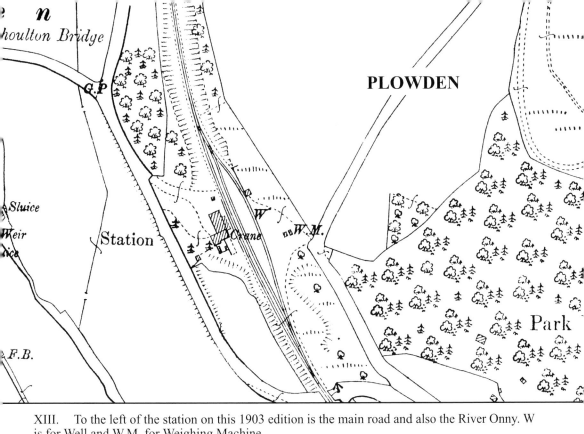

XIII.   To the left of the station on this 1903 edition is the main road and also the River Onny. W is for Well and W.M. for Weighing Machine.

54.   This is the east elevation in October 1931, with coal awaiting delivery locally. A demurrage charge on wagons necessitated their speedy emptying. A GPO letter box is evident in the wall. (R.S.Carpenter coll.)

55.   The prospective passenger's perspective was recorded in 1958, much as it was in 1935. This elevation could still be seen from the A489 fifty years after the photograph was taken. (R.M.Casserley)

56.   In 1905, the BCR purchased a 40-year old 517 class 0-4-2T from the GWR and it became no. 1, a quaint decision. It is about to be cut up, shortly after line closure, along with some wagons and carriage frames. The bodies of some coaches had been sold as holiday homes. *Carlisle* is shunting the relics. (R.C.Anthony)

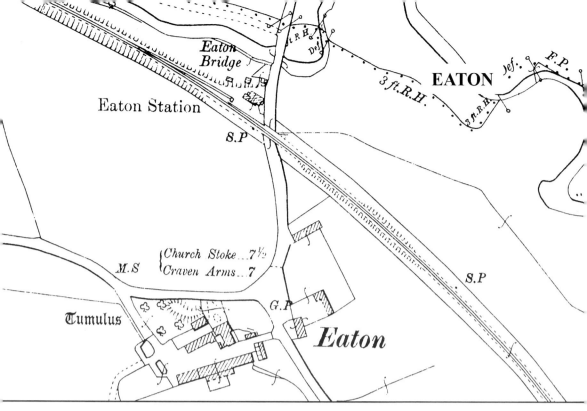

Map labels:
Eaton Bridge
EATON
Eaton Station
3 ft.R.H.
S.P
{ Church Stoke...7½
{ Craven Arms...7
M.S
Tumulus
G.P
S.P
Eaton

XIV.   Again the River Onny is evident on another 1903 extract, but there are very few dwellings nearby. This still applies.

57.   The station was "maintained" by a lone lady during its final 25 years or so, with improvisation being the basic requirement of the post. (R.M.Casserley coll.)

58.　　The track was appalling and one of the many dropped joints can be seen on the right. However, the siding can hardly be seen at all; it ends at the sleeper barrier.
(R.M.Casserley coll.)

59.　　This was almost always a request stop and the signal arm was used to indicate the presence of an intending passenger. It seems that the wire had broken by the time the photographer had arrived on 8th October 1931.
(R.S.Carpenter coll.)

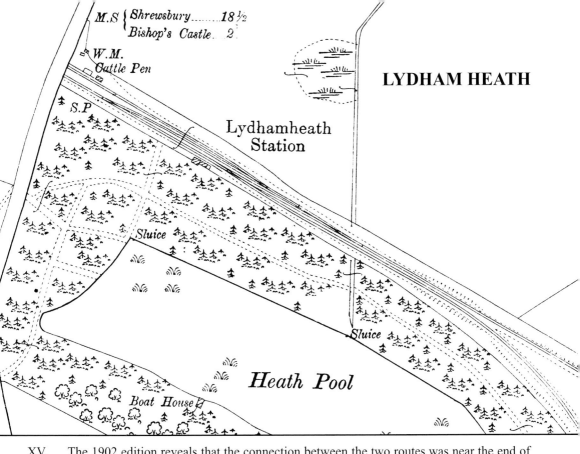

M.S { Shrewsbury........18½
     { Bishop's Castle. 2

W.M.
Cattle Pen

S.P

LYDHAM HEATH

Lydhamheath
Station

Sluice

Sluice

Heath Pool

Boat House

XV.   The 1902 edition reveals that the connection between the two routes was near the end of the platform.

60.   A new building was erected here in 1906; this is its predecessor, with the gents on the left. The new one still had no staff accommodation, but first and second class waiting rooms were provided. The covering of sleepers had been prohibited long before this date on other railways. (R.M.Casserley coll.)

61.   An eastward view from the end of the line in 1931 appears to include tools lying near the point. There were two small gangs, but most of their work involved cutting back lineside trees. (R.S.Carpenter coll.)

→   62. This is the 11.20am from Craven Arms on 30th May 1932 and it is about to change direction for the final leg of its journey. Most coaches were reported as decrepit; this is one of the best and is ex-Hull & Barnsley Railway. (H.C.Casserley)

Issued by the B. C. Ry, subject to the conditions in their Time Tables

THIRD CLASS

BISHOP'S CASTLE   To

LYDHAM HEATH

2478

Lydham Heath   Fare 4½d

→   63. This station was reputed to have been the only one on the railway to have a clock that worked, in the final years. No ballast was used when the track was laid and a report in the 1920s stated that trees were cut from nearby land when replacement sleepers were required. (Stations UK)

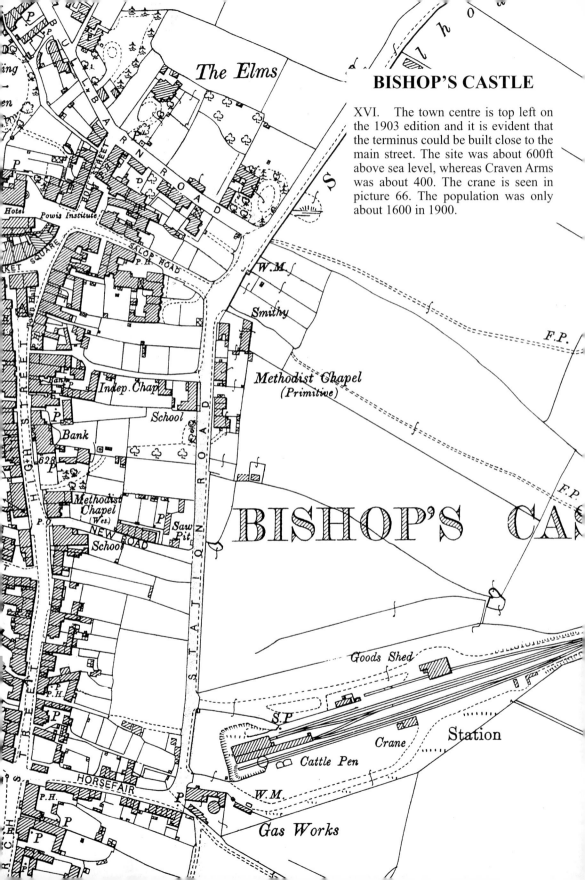

The Elms

BISHOP'S CASTLE

XVI. The town centre is top left on the 1903 edition and it is evident that the terminus could be built close to the main street. The site was about 600ft above sea level, whereas Craven Arms was about 400. The crane is seen in picture 66. The population was only about 1600 in 1900.

Hotel

Powis Institute

SALOP ROAD

W.M.

Smithy

Methodist Chapel
(Primitive)

Indep. Chap.

School

Bank

Bank

628

Methodist
Chapel
(Wes.)

P.O.

NEW ROAD

Saw
Pit

School

STATION ROAD

HIGH STREET

F.P.

F.P.

BISHOP'S CA

Goods Shed

S.P.

Crane

Station

Cattle Pen

W.M.

HORSEFAIR

Gas Works

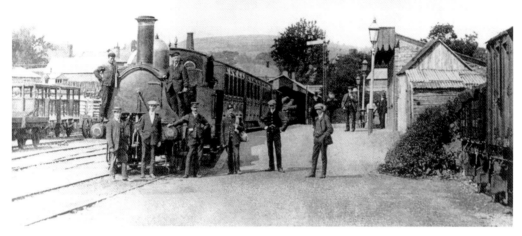

64.   An early postcard features BCR no. 1 and so it must be after 1905. The 0-4-2T had been built in 1869 and had been GWR no. 567. The cattle wagons are near the dock. (P.Q.Treloar coll.)

65.   A westward view from about 1906 has the station approach road in the background and the engine shed on the left. Parliamentary tickets were issued to the end; this was lower than 3rd class. (R.M.Casserley coll.)

66.   The BCR had seven locomotives during its existence and these were the final two. No. 1 has been described; on the right is *Carlisle*, which had been built by Kitson in 1868 for a contractor. It was purchased by the BCR in 1895. (P.Q.Treloar coll.)

Issued by the **BISHOP'S CASTLE RY. CO.,** subject to the Conditions & Regulations set out in the Company's Time Tables, Bills and Notices.
COVERNMENT RATE
TICKET.
POLICEMAN ON DUTY
BISHOP'S CASTLE   To
CRAVEN ARMS
790

Issued by the B. C. Ry. subject to the conditions in their Time Tables
PARLIAMENTARY
BISHOP'S CASTLE   To
EATON
Eaton   Fare -/6
2110
14DC

Issued by the B. C. Ry. subject to the conditions in their Time Tables
PARLIAMENTARY
BISHOP'S CASTLE   To
PLOWDEN
Plowden   Fare -/9½
1491

Issued by the B. C. Ry. subject to the conditions in their Time Tables
PARLIAMENTARY
BISHOP'S CASTLE   To
PLOWDEN
Plowden   Fare /8½
0549

67.   The company's road transport included a steam wagon and a 14-seater Chevrolet bus. The station had no chimneys - another economy measure. (R.S.Carpenter coll.)

68.   A departure is imminent on 30th May 1932; few other coaches had their ends sprayed with mud. This one was reported as ex-LSWR. (H.C.Casserley)

69.   This was probably the last railway to operate without continuous brakes and thus the order of the vehicles was of no consequence. This is the same train and it is due to leave at 12.40 behind *Carlisle*. (H.C.Casserley)

70.   No. 1 is in the shed on the same day. Propped up on the left is the carriage shed. The signal position is certainly unorthodox. (H.C.Casserley)

71.   A snap inside the shed soon after closure has no. 1 at the back. *Carlisle* originally ran with a four-wheeled tender; this is an ex-GWR model. Staff working conditions were basic in the extreme. (P.Q.Treloar coll.)

72.   The goods shed and station building were retained after closure, but the engine and carriage sheds were demolished. Seen in 1963, the goods office was the only one to have a chimney. (R.M.Casserley)

CRAVEN ARMS

Stone

M.P.

S.P.

Union & R.D. Bdy.

*Newington
House*

Lodge

Newing

Newi.
Terr

S.P.
B

Allotment
Gardens

*Newington
Villa*

Smithy

Newi

S.P.

Def.

F.W.

Def.

*Allotm
Gard.*

F.J.

XVII. The 1903 map has the main road of the Borders (A49 since 1919) on the right. Long Lane is the turning from it and the crossing box adjacent to it was so named until 1956, when it became "Craven Arms Crossing". Its gates were replaced by barriers in 1969. The term "Crossing" was dropped in 1965, when Junction box closed. The goods yard continues on the next extract. The transverse siding has only one wagon turntable marked, whereas railway records show four. The villages of Newington and Newtown expanded and joined following the creation of the railway junction and the name, it seems, became that of the inn between them. The travelling crane was for timber traffic and two private sidings were laid to the east of it. They were used by South Shropshire Farmers Ltd from 1931 to 1968.

F.P.

W.M.

S.P.

Travelling Crane

6

274

*Cattle
Pens*

F.P.

S.P.

S.P.

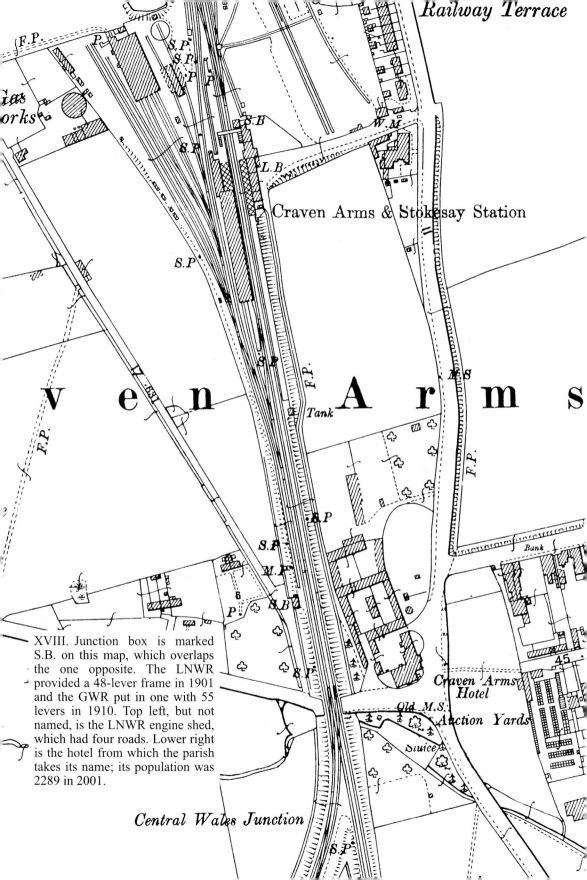

Railway Terrace

F.P.   P   S.P.
    S.P.
    P

Gas Works

S.B.

S.P.

W.M.

L.B.

Craven Arms & Stokesay Station

S.P.

F.P.

S.P.

v e n **A r m s**

F.P.   Tank

F.P.

F.P.

S.P.

M.S.

S.P.

M.F.

Bank

P   S.B.

4.5

XVIII. Junction box is marked
S.B. on this map, which overlaps
the one opposite. The LNWR
provided a 48-lever frame in 1901
and the GWR put in one with 55
levers in 1910. Top left, but not
named, is the LNWR engine shed,
which had four roads. Lower right
is the hotel from which the parish
takes its name; its population was
2289 in 2001.

Craven Arms
Hotel

Old M.S.
Auction Yards

Sluice

Central Wales Junction

S.P.

73.   The LNWR operated the Central Wales line and most of its trains terminated in the bay platform on the left of this view, which is from the early 1920s. (Stations UK)

74.   North Bay is on the right, but it was not always authorised for use by passenger trains. On the left is part of Station Box, which had a 33-lever frame from about 1911 until closure on 26th March 1956. (Lens of Sutton coll.)

75.   GWR steam railmotor no. 74 is about to depart north with two coaches for the Much Wenlock branch. The lower signals are for the north bay. (R.S.Carpenter coll.)

76.   The full length of North Bay is evident in this view from about 1906. A double-framed GWR 0-6-0 runs in from the north and almost obscures the signal box. The bay was used by trains to Bishop's Castle. (G.M.Perkins/R.S.Carpenter coll.)

77. The 10.10am Shrewsbury to Hereford runs in on 10th September 1949 behind no. 5097 *Sarum Castle*. Arrival was at 11.1 - two stops were missed on the 20-mile journey. (H.C.Casserley)

→ 78. A glimpse of the goods yard is obtained in 1949 before the BR "Lion & Monocycle" logo was applied to 2-4-2T no. 46727. The LNWR introduced this class in 1890. Cattle wagons are in the right background. (B.W.L.Brooksbank)

```
  G.W.&L.&N.W.Jt.    G.W.&L.&N.W.Jt.
  CRAVEN ARMS        CRAVEN ARMS
  & STOKESAY         & STOKESAY
    (S.00)       TO
     CHURCH STRETTON
        7d THIRD CLASS 7d
    Issued subject to the conditions and
    Regulations set out in the Companies
    Time Tables, Bills & Notices.  (BL)
     Church Stretton    Church Stretton
```
1241 1241

→ 79. A northward panorama from North Bay in August 1951 features the six-road carriage shed, to the left of which is the white area of the turntable pit. (R.G.Nelson/T.Walsh)

80.   No. 42307 waits to leave for the Central Wales line on 11th April 1955, while sister engine no. 42385 arrives from Hereford. The station still had a refreshment room at this time. The timber yard in the background had its own siding from 1922 to 1965. (G.Adams/M.J.Stretton coll.)

→   81. No. 45145 is working a Shrewsbury to Swansea Victoria service on 31st March 1962. The station had the suffix "& Stokesay" from July 1879 until May 1974. (H.Ballantyne)

→   82. No. 5056 *Earl of Powis* is bound for Cardiff on 5th June 1964. The goods yard had a 5-ton crane, but all freight traffic ceased on 6th May 1968. (D.Johnson)

83.   The 12.25 from Swansea on 17th July 1976 leaves the third track; this was dedicated to Central Wales trains. The line curves west beyond the fourth telephone pole behind the train. The junction had been in that vicinity until 12th December 1965. The route is now "The Heart of Wales Line". (T.Heavyside)

→ 84. On the left is the carriage shed, which was little used after the end of steam here in 1965. The 10.11 from Swansea is approaching the level crossing and its signal box on 15th August 1984. The crossover is immediately in front of the train. The box had a new upper section in 1947, plus a frame of 30 levers. (D.H.Mitchell)

→ 85. No. 158830 is southbound on 18th March 2004. Nothing remained of the old station except the goods shed, which is visible in the background. An extra entrance on the west side had been provided for new housing development. (M.Turvey)

Craven Arms
Engine Shed

↑ 86. The number of tracks in the depot was reduced from four to three in the mid-1930s. We have two photographs from 22nd April 1957. This features no. 49117, by then of class G2a and rated as 7F. The prototype was built by the LNWR in 1892.
(G.Adams/M.J.Stretton coll.)

↗ 87. No. 43679 (left) was an 0-6-0 of the type introduced by the Midland Railway in 1885. Nos 9004 and 9024 were GWR 4-4-0s produced from 1936 onwards.
(G.Adams/M.J.Stretton coll.)

→ 88. Another ex-GWR locomotive was present when our photographer arrived on 18th May 1961. Also included are the premises built by the Craven Arms Gas Company.
(R.G.Nelson/T.Walsh)

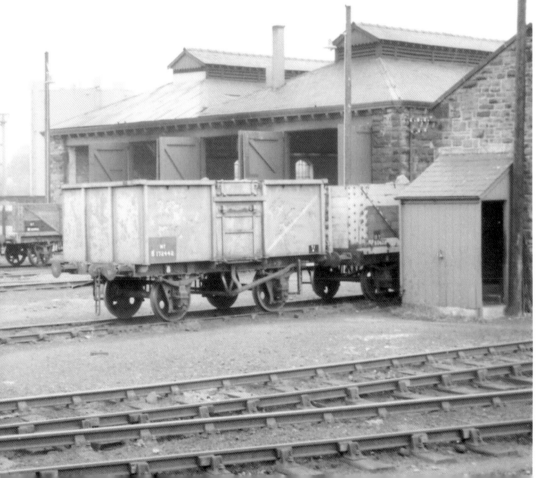

89.   This northward panorama includes Stokesay Castle, which is of 13th century origin and was owned by the Lords Craven. No. 33030 is heading the 16.02 Crewe to Cardiff on 4th April 1983. (T.Heavyside)

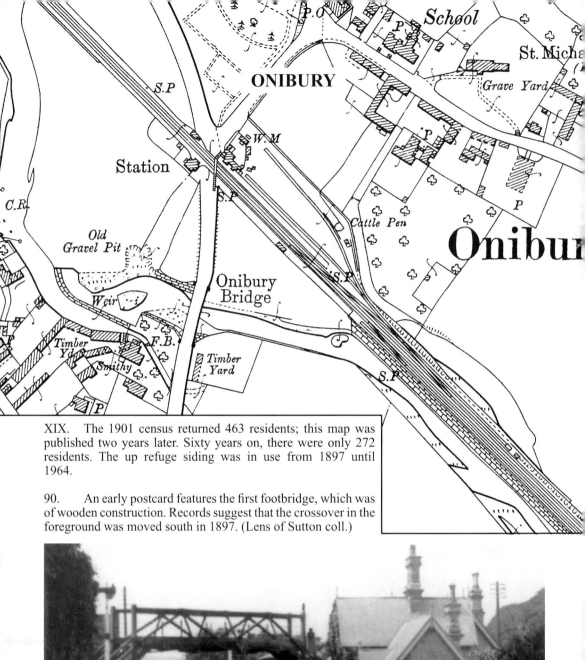

XIX.   The 1901 census returned 463 residents; this map was published two years later. Sixty years on, there were only 272 residents. The up refuge siding was in use from 1897 until 1964.

90.   An early postcard features the first footbridge, which was of wooden construction. Records suggest that the crossover in the foreground was moved south in 1897. (Lens of Sutton coll.)

91.   The steel lattice replacement bridge gave much improved visibility for the signalman. Both goods and passenger services were withdrawn here on 9th June 1958, the year in which this photograph was taken. (Stations UK)

92.   The northward view from the footbridge in 1961 includes the complex rodding for gate operation. The box closed on 12th December 1977; it had 24 levers. (R.G.Nelson/T.Walsh)

93.	A 1963 panorama includes the site for the 1977 replacement signal box, left. The building seen subsequently housed popular tea rooms for many years. (H.C.Casserley)

94.	Lifting barriers had appeared and the footbridge removed by the time no. 6000 *King George V* was recorded on 27th October 1973 obstructing the A49. (T.Heavyside)

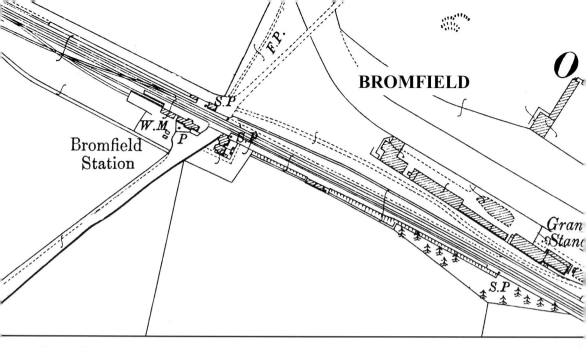

XX.   The 1903 survey shows staggered platforms, with the down one west of the level crossing. A new and longer one was provided east thereof, in about 1904. The local population fell from 625 in 1901 to 365 in 1961.

95.   A westward panorama from around 1935 has the new platform and Ludlow Racecourse on the left. Records of racing here go back to 1729, but it probably started in the 14th century. (Stations UK)

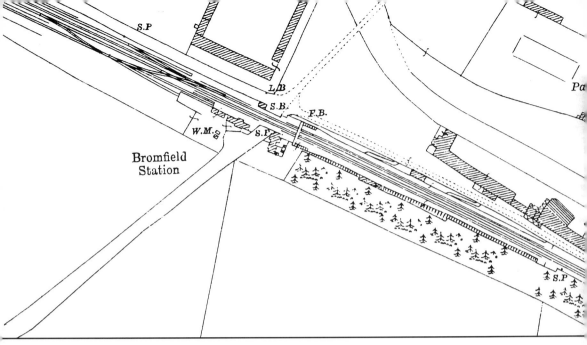

XXI.   The 1926 edition reveals that the original down platform had been replaced by a refuge siding. Alongside it is a long platform for horse traffic. Now a National Hunt course, it did not have jumping until the mid-19th century.

96.   Seen from the second up platform is the original short one, which was adjacent to the main building. The photograph is from 1958; passenger service ceased here on 9th June of that year. (Stations UK/J.Peden)

97.   Seen in 1961, the platforms remained in use for race traffic for some years. The only remaining sign was for the benefit of gentlemen. The village was ½ mile to the south. (R.G.Nelson/T.Walsh)

98.   Working a northbound special on 18th August 1963 is no. 6877 *Llanfair Grange*. We view it from the long horse platform. The adjacent track had become a loop in July 1941 and was still serving as such. (B.W.L.Brooksbank)

99.   From a similar viewpoint in the same year, we see much of the goods yard, which was in use until 15th June 1964. It had a 5-ton crane listed in 1938. (H.C.Casserley)

100.   The stops on the right are on the horse dock siding. The two staff dwellings are on the opposite side of the road to the main building. (R.M.Casserley)

101. Our views of the box are from May 1989, when the down loop was still in use. Full lifting barriers had replaced the gates on 18th November 1975. There were water troughs south of here in the later steam days. (P.G.Barnes)

102. The WR installed this 29-lever frame in April 1956, it replacing a 1900 LNWR unit containing 23-levers. The white levers are out of use and the push buttons on the left are for barrier control. (P.G.Barnes)

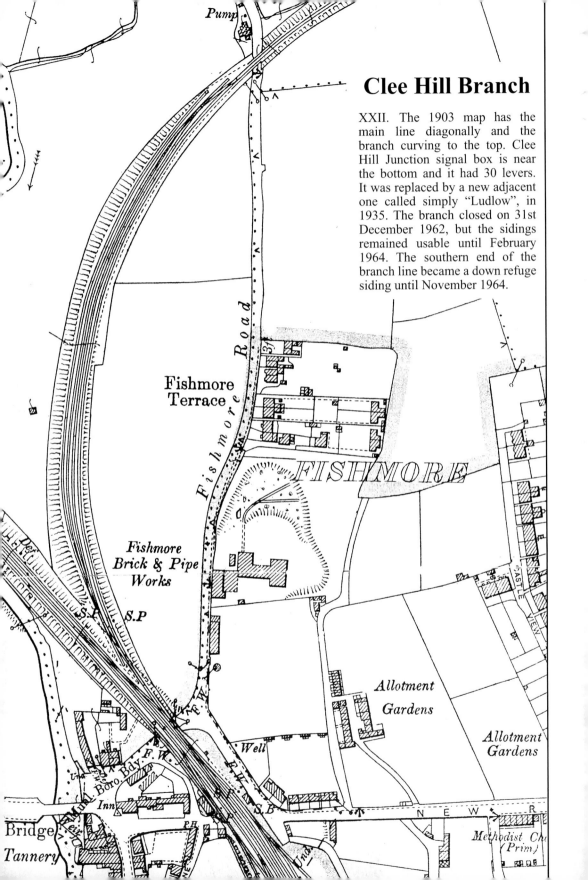

Clee Hill Branch

XXII. The 1903 map has the main line diagonally and the branch curving to the top. Clee Hill Junction signal box is near the bottom and it had 30 levers. It was replaced by a new adjacent one called simply "Ludlow", in 1935. The branch closed on 31st December 1962, but the sidings remained usable until February 1964. The southern end of the branch line became a down refuge siding until November 1964.

Fishmore Terrace

FISHMORE

Fishmore Road

Fishmore Brick & Pipe Works

S.P   S.P

Well

Allotment Gardens

Allotment Gardens

CASTLE VIEW

Pump

NEW R

Bridge

Tannery

Inn

Methodist Ch (Prim)

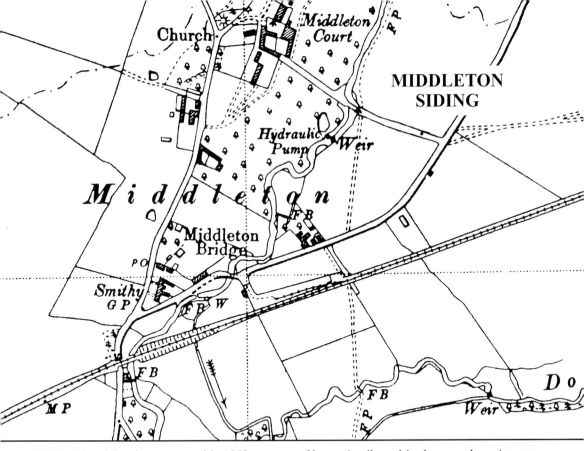

XXIII. The siding is centre on this 1952 survey at 3ins to 1 mile and is shown to have its own access road. This was gated, as was the siding, although it was listed as for public traffic.

103.   A March 1961 photograph shows some wagons loaded with coal and the points in the distance. There had been an end and side loading dock here earlier. (J.Langford)

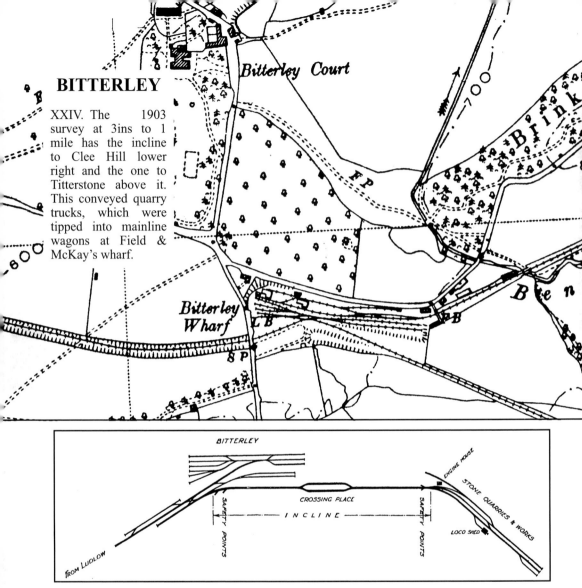

BITTERLEY

XXIV. The 1903 survey at 3ins to 1 mile has the incline to Clee Hill lower right and the one to Titterstone above it. This conveyed quarry trucks, which were tipped into mainline wagons at Field & McKay's wharf.

Bitterley Court

Bitterley Wharf

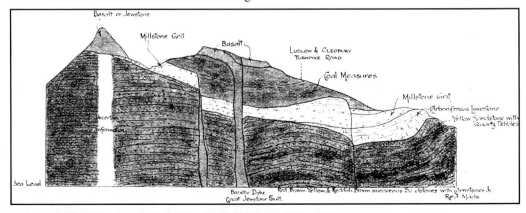

XXV. Diagram from 1923. (GWR Magazine)

XXVI. A sketch from the 1920s indicates the geology of Titterstone Clee Hill. The Basalt or Jewstone was also known as Dhustone. It had been oozed out as molten material and was granite-like in hardness and thus ideal for road making.

104.   The view east from the road bridge in 1955 features the lower end of the Clee Hill Incline. Beyond the signal box are two level sidings and on the left is the line which climbs up steeply to Bitterley Wharf, where there was a crushing plant. (T.J.Edgington)

105.   Three closer views of the junction in September 1960 show details and levels. Empty wagons stand on the Ludlow line, as 0-6-0PT no. 3602 uses the headshunt, which had once been part of a loop. (H.C.Casserley)

106.   No. 3602 is hauling loaded wagons from the upper sidings. The 1907 signal box had for long been used as a ground frame. The lean of the lamp post increased over the years. (H.C.Casserley)

107.   Pulleys in both planes were required on the curve. The limit of the weedkiller is evident. There was a workmens service between here and Ludlow in 1905, calling at Middleton Siding. (R.M.Casserley)

→   XXVII. On the left of the 1903 map is the top of the incline. Near the bottom is the engine shed; the tracks to this were altered later and a smaller structure was erected. The branch was conveying around 6000 tons of road stone per week in the early 1920s.

→   108 Standing outside the well-propped shed in about 1950 is LMS no. 7164, a vertical-boilered Sentinel, one of a small batch built in 1928-30. (It was 7184 on most records.) Horses were used on this top level until 1877. (P.Q.Treloar coll.)

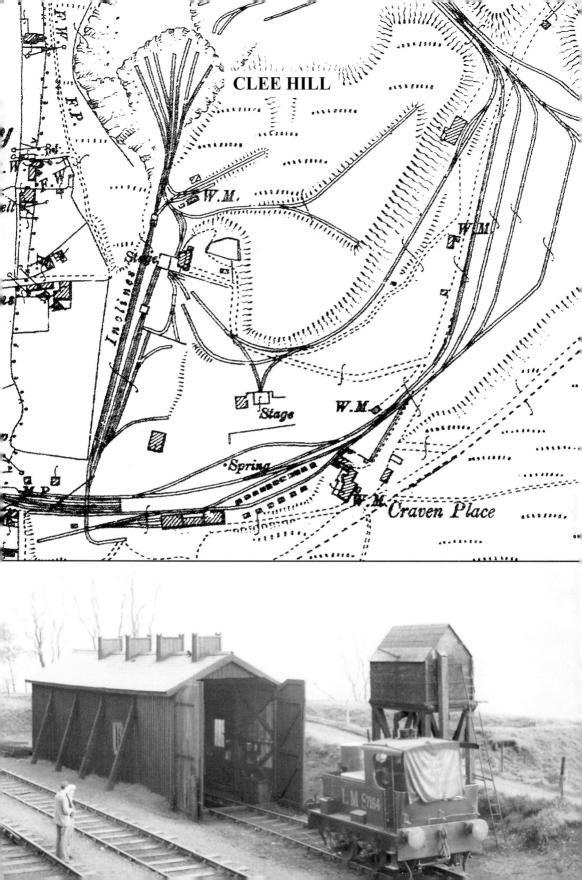

CLEE HILL

W.M.

W.M.

Incline Stage

W.M.

Stage

Spring

W.M. Craven Place

L.M.S. 7164

109.　The incline was 1720yds in length and regarded as the longest standard gauge one in Britain. We look towards the top of it in April 1955. The sidings branching from the three rails were to catch runaways. (T.J.Edgington)

110.　Ex-Swansea Harbour Trust 0-4-0ST no. 1142 is shunting at Clee Hill summit on 15th August 1958. It was built by Hudswell Clarke in 1911 and this was its GWR number. Trains of empty wagons were divided at Middleton Siding, owing to a 1 in 26 gradient east to Bitterley. (B.Morrison)

111.　A view down the incline emphasises its length, but does not include its four-rail section at the mid-point. The gradient was 1 in 9.27. The steel rope had six strands, each of which had 21 wires. The maximum load was 85 tons. (J.Langford)

112.   Turning round, we see the return to four rails and witness the ropes passing under the rails to the brake house. The brake blocks were wooden and lasted six years. This and the final two photographs are from September 1960, two months before closure. (R.M.Casserley)

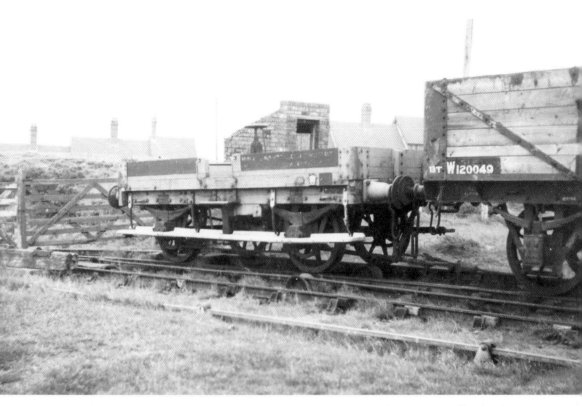

113.   This unusual brake truck was used on the incline and has been seen earlier in pictures 105-107. Behind it is a classically ventilated privy. The wagon was known as "The Dummy" and was always attached to the rope. (R.M.Casserley)

114.   We have a final look back at the engine shed, left. On the right are the premises of ARC Ltd. This windswept location was 1250ft above sea level. A public goods service was provided here to the end; the goods shed may be in picture 110. (H.C.Casserley)

Fishmore Road Works
(Brick & Pipe)
Kilns
S.P.
Old
Brickyar

LUDLOW

XXVIII. The 1st edition is from 1886, when the town still had several malthouses, a brewery and a workhouse. The cattle market was conveniently close to the station. The track layout changed little, apart from the removal of the transverse sidings in the 1950s.

Union Wor

Signal Box
Inn
B.M. 303·7
B.M. 277
B.M.
Engine Shed
Alnshouses
Goods Shed
Reservo
P.H.
W.M.
Maltho.
Inn Maltho
Maltho.
Brick
Field
Kiln
Almshouses
(A.D. 1500)

Other views can be seen in pictures 1 to 7 in our *Ludlow to Hereford* album.

Monastery
(Carmelite)
Stone House
St Leonard's
Church
ve Yard
Site of
Leonards Ch
B.M. 291·5
Cattle
Pens
S.P.
STATION DRIVE
Cattle Pens
B.M.
Station
Auction
Mart
L.B.
B.M. 293·4
Brewery
Inn
Kiln
S.P.
Brick Works

115. A view north from the footbridge in the early 1930s includes Ludlow Station signal box, which closed in 1935. (Mowat coll./Brunel University)

116. There was a local service between Tenbury Wells and Ludlow, reversing at Woofferton, and it was often worked by 0-4-2Ts, such as no. 1445. The train was used mainly by school pupils and is seen on 3rd June 1961. It also appears in our *Branch Lines around Cleobury Mortimer*. (G.Adams/M.J.Stretton coll.)

117.   Three photographs from July 1964 create a comprehensive survey. A southward view features the portal of the 132yd long Ludlow Tunnel. (Lens of Sutton coll.)

118.   The up platform was cluttered with stanchions, a feature avoided on most GWR stations, where cantilevered trusses were used. The buildings were destroyed in the late 1960s and the gas lights were lost at that time. (Lens of Sutton coll.)

119.   A panorama from above the tunnel mouth includes much of the goods yard, which closed on 6th May 1968. The engine shed had been in the right distance and was in use until December 1951. (Lens of Sutton coll.)

120.   No. 158835 calls whilst southbound on 18th March 2004 and stops near one of the improved waiting shelters. The up side had better buildings by that time; only the goods shed (left) stood as a link with the past. (M.Turvey)

MP **Middleton Press**

EVOLVING THE ULTIMATE RAIL ENCYCLOPEDIA

Easebourne Lane, Midhurst, West Sussex.
GU29 9AZ   Tel:01730 813169

www.middletonpress.co.uk   email:info@middletonpress.co.uk
A-978 0 906520 B- 978 1 873793 C-978 1 901706 D-978 1 904474 E - 978 1 906008

OOP Out of print at time of printing - Please check availability   BROCHURE AVAILABLE SHOWING NEW TITLES